D1514747

7-20

DESHAUN WATSON

SUPERSTAR QUARTERBACK

BIG BUDDY

★ NFL ★

SUPERSTARS

Big Buddy Books

An Imprint of Abdo Publishing
abdobooks.com

DENNIS ST. SAUVER

abdobooks.com

Published by Abdo Publishing, a division of ABDO, PO Box 398166, Minneapolis, Minnesota 55439.
Copyright © 2020 by Abdo Consulting Group, Inc. International copyrights reserved in all countries.
No part of this book may be reproduced in any form without written permission from the publisher.
Big Buddy Books™ is a trademark and logo of Abdo Publishing.

Printed in the United States of America, North Mankato, Minnesota.
052019
092019

Cover Photo: efks/Getty Images; Tim Warner/Getty Images.
Interior Photos: Bob Levey/Getty Images (pp. 17, 19, 23, 29); Bobby Ellis/Getty Images (p. 5); Jason
    Getz/AP Images (p. 11); Joe Robbins/Getty Images (p. 15); Joyce Marshall/AP Images (p. 27);
    Mark Stehle/AP Images (p. 25); Mitchell Leff/Getty Images (p. 9); Streeter Lecka/Getty Images
    (p. 13); Tim Warner/Getty Images (p. 21).

Coordinating Series Editor: Elizabeth Andrews
Graphic Design: Jenny Christensen, Cody Laberda

Library of Congress Control Number: 2018967168

Publisher's Cataloging-in-Publication Data

Names: St. Sauver, Dennis, author.
Title: Deshaun Watson: superstar quarterback / by Dennis St. Sauver
Other title: Superstar quarterback
Description: Minneapolis, Minnesota : Abdo Publishing, 2020 | Series: NFL superstars |
    Includes online resources and index.
Identifiers: ISBN 9781532119859 (lib. bdg.) | ISBN 9781532174612 (ebook)
Subjects: LCSH: Quarterbacks (Football)--United States--Biography--Juvenile literature. |
    Football players--United States--Biography--Juvenile literature. | Houston Texans (Football
    team)--Juvenile literature. | Sports--Biography--Juvenile literature.
Classification: DDC 796.3326409 [B]--dc23

CONTENTS

★ ★ ★ ★ ★ ★

SUPERSTAR QUARTERBACK

Deshaun Watson is a quarterback in the National Football League (NFL). He plays for the Houston Texans in Texas. By his second year in the NFL, he had become one of the most exciting players in the league.

DID YOU KNOW?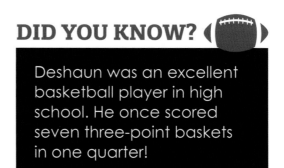

Deshaun was an excellent basketball player in high school. He once scored seven three-point baskets in one quarter!

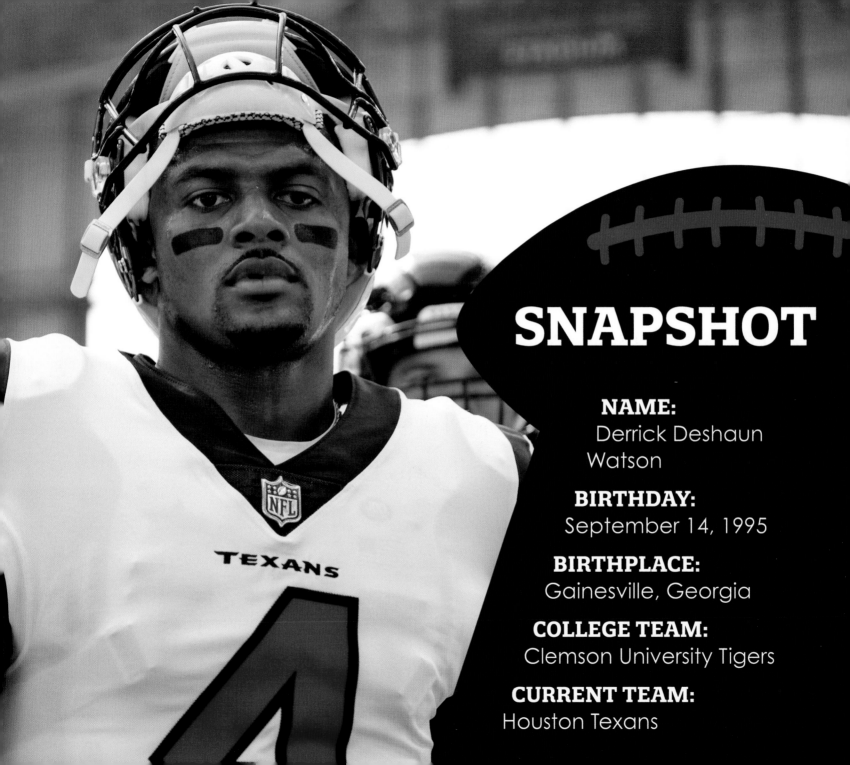

SNAPSHOT

NAME:
Derrick Deshaun Watson

BIRTHDAY:
September 14, 1995

BIRTHPLACE:
Gainesville, Georgia

COLLEGE TEAM:
Clemson University Tigers

CURRENT TEAM:
Houston Texans

EARLY YEARS

Deshaun's mother is Deann Watson. He has an older brother named Detrick. He also has a brother and sister who are twins. Their names are Tyreka and Tinisha. Deshaun is very close to his aunt and uncle, Sonia and Terri.

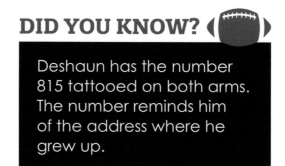

DID YOU KNOW?

Deshaun has the number 815 tattooed on both arms. The number reminds him of the address where he grew up.

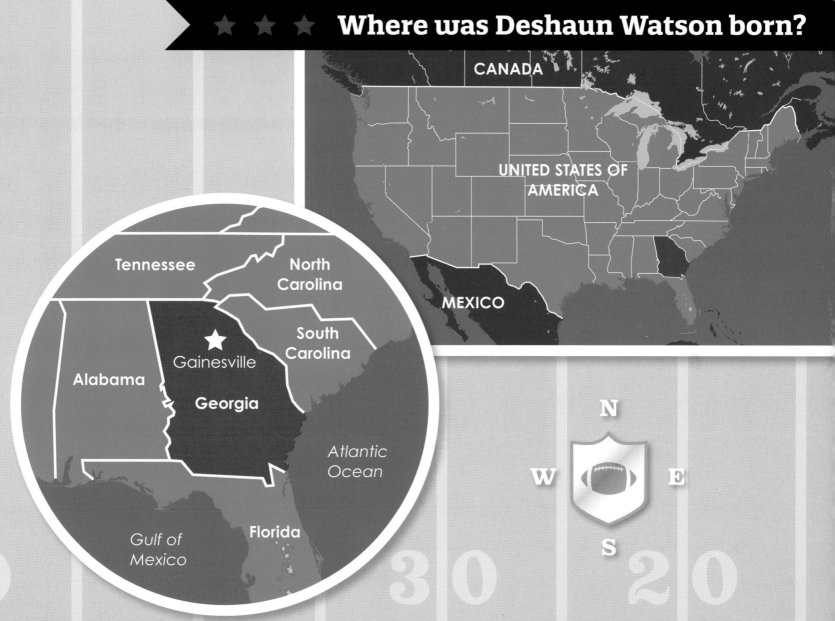

Where was Deshaun Watson born?

CANADA

UNITED STATES OF AMERICA

MEXICO

Tennessee

North Carolina

South Carolina

Alabama

★ Gainesville

Georgia

Atlantic Ocean

Gulf of Mexico

Florida

N
W E
S

STARTING OUT

Deshaun attended Gainesville High School in Georgia. He became the starting quarterback when he was a freshman. By the end of his freshman season, Deshaun finished with more than 2,000 **passing** yards (1,829 m).

As a junior, he led the team to the Class 5A State **Championship**. Deshaun finished the game with 400 total yards (366 m) of offense and five touchdowns. Gainesville won the championship!

Deshaun brought his mother Deann *(left)* and his aunt Sonia *(right)* to the 2017 NFL Draft red carpet event.

★ ★ ★ ★ ★ ★ ★ ★

The victory marked Gainesville's first state **championship** in the school's 100-year history. Deshaun ended his junior season with more than 4,000 **passing** yards (3,658 m).

Deshaun **graduated** from Gainesville in 2014. He finished his high school **career** with more than 13,000 total passing yards (11,887 m).

In 2012, Deshaun set the state record for total touchdowns. By the time he finished high school he had 218 touchdowns.

BIG DREAMS

After high school, Deshaun went to Clemson University in South Carolina. There, he was **nominated** for the **Heisman Trophy** twice!

In his third season, he led his team to the College Football **Playoff** National **Championship**. Clemson won against the number one team and **rival**, the Alabama Crimson Tide, in the last seconds of the game.

Deshaun finished his college career with more than 10,000 passing yards (9,144 m) and 90 touchdowns.

GOING PRO

In 2017, the Houston Texans **drafted** Deshaun. He was the twelfth overall pick in the first round.

The season was going well for the team until Deshaun was **injured**. The Texans finished with only four wins and 12 losses. Deshaun's team needed him back on the field.

In 2017, Deshaun earned the AFC Offensive Player of the Month Award. He made NFL history as the first rookie quarterback to earn the award.

Deshaun was a star for the Texans in 2018. He became an **elite** quarterback in the league. And he led his team to the AFC South **Division title**.

As a quarterback, Deshaun is able to throw, scramble, and run. This makes him a very **valuable** player for the Texans. He even came in at number 50 on the 2018 NFL Top 100 players list.

DID YOU KNOW?

Deshaun once found a $20 bill and turned it in to his coach instead of keeping it for himself.

The Texans wide receiver DeAndre Hopkins (right) thinks Deshaun is a great quarterback. DeAndre once said, "I wouldn't want any other quarterback in this entire universe other than him."

A RISING STAR

Deshaun's first year in the NFL was very successful. In 2017, he threw five touchdowns in a single game, setting his personal record.

In 2018, the Texans had an excellent start. The players wanted to make it to the **playoffs.** By the end of the regular season, the team had won the **division title**!

In addition to 26 passing touchdowns, Deshaun scored five rushing touchdowns in 2018.

Deshaun continues to amaze players and fans with his skills. He has set several records since joining the Texans.

He set an amazing NFL record in 2017. Deshaun **passed** for 400 yards (366 m), got four touchdowns, and **rushed** for 50 yards (46 m) in one game. He also led his team to its first season of ten or more wins since 2012.

The young quarterback threw a touchdown in his very first NFL game.

OFF THE FIELD

Deshaun and his family did not have a lot of money when he was growing up. When he was 11 years old, past NFL player Warrick Dunn **donated** a home to Deshaun's family. It was through a program called Habitat for Humanity. He never forgot the wonderful gift.

DID YOU KNOW?

Deshaun is the first member of his family to graduate from college. And he did it in only three years!

In 2016, Deshaun won the Johnny Unitas Golden Arm Award. The award is given to the nation's best senior quarterback in college football.

GIVING BACK

Deshaun never forgot what others did for him growing up. He **donated** his first NFL paycheck to three cafeteria employees. They were dealing with the effects of Hurricane Harvey in 2017.

Deshaun also **supports** Habitat for Humanity. While in college, he and his teammates helped build homes for families in need.

In 2017, Deshaun and Carson Wentz (*center left*) co-hosted an event along with JCPenney. The event was held to help young men prepare for their futures.

AWARDS

Deshaun has won many awards during his football **career**. He was a USA TODAY High School Sports **All-American** in 2013. And he was named an All-American at Clemson. There, he also earned the ACC Player of the Year Award in 2015.

He won ESPN's Best Male College Athlete ESPY Award in 2017. And he is a two-time Davey O'Brien Award winner.

The Davey O'Brien Award is given each year to the best college quarterback in the NCAA.

BUZZ

Deshaun has been an amazing quarterback for his team. His coaches and teammates expect that he will continue delivering wins for the Texans. Fans are excited to see what he does next!

DID YOU KNOW?

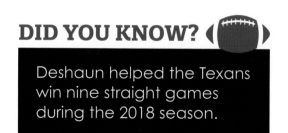

Deshaun helped the Texans win nine straight games during the 2018 season.

Deshaun finished the 2018 regular season with 4,165 passing yards (3,808 m) and 551 rushing yards (503 m).

GLOSSARY

All-American selected as one of the best in the US in a particular sport.

career a period of time spent in a certain job.

championship a game, a match, or a race held to find a first-place winner.

division a number of teams grouped together in a sport for competitive purposes.

donate giving something to help those in need.

draft a system for professional sports teams to choose new players.

elite superior in quality, rank, or skill.

graduate (GRA-juh-wayt) to complete a level of schooling.

Heisman Trophy (HAIS-muhn TROH-fee) an award given each year to the most outstanding player in college football.

injure (IHN-juhr) to cause pain or harm.

nominate to name as a possible winner.

pass to throw the football in the direction of the opponent's goal.

playoffs a game or series of games to determine a championship or break a tie.

rival one who competes for the same position as another.

rush to advance a football by running plays.

support to provide help or encouragement to.

title a first-place position in a contest.

valuable of great use or service.

ONLINE RESOURCES

Booklinks
NONFICTION NETWORK
FREE! ONLINE NONFICTION RESOURCES

To learn more about Deshaun Watson, please visit **abdobooklinks.com** or scan this QR code. These links are routinely monitored and updated to provide the most current information available.

★ ★ ★ INDEX ★ ★ ★